The Moving Landmarks

MIKE CLARK

The Moving Landmarks

First published in Great Britain in 2021 by Mike Clark

Email: m.e.clark@hotmail.com

ISBN: 979-850951-238-4

Artwork by Sally Ireland

Page layout by Reach Publishing: info@wearereach.org

CONTENTS

ACKNOWLEDGEMENTS

In my first book of poems my middle son Luke kindly enabled me to organise and make my poems presentable. In the present volume it is because of the strong encouragement and persistence of my third son Nathaniel that I have submitted this work to publication. (My eldest son Jamie would pay me not to be included, so I have decided to accept the money!)

I am also indebted to my friends John Richards and Johnathan Badcock for their kind responses encouragement and suggestions.

FOREWORD

In the preface to my first book of poems I raised the fact that an eye condition had severely curtailed the amount of reading I was capable of doing which had limited the breadth of my studies. In the period between these publications I have discovered a wonderful healing secret that has
restored my reading ability to near normality. I am therefore left without excuse!

Poems are like photographs. They convey and represent a perspective of reality at a given moment, but time marches on. Some of our perspectives change, but tomorrow's perceptions do not invalidate yesterday's experiences!

In this volume I have decided to include a biographical note describing, where appropriate, the context in which the poems were written.

INTRODUCTION

That I should find myself writing a book of poetry is almost unbelievable to me. Growing up in the 60's and 70's, and having an interest in song-writing, it was inevitable that I would have a flirtation with composing verse, but it was nearly disastrous! It was heavy, laboured and mechanical - a source of potential embarrassment! This was in my teens and early twenties, but then at the age of 30 a career defining event took place.

I was a teacher in a small private stage school. Employed on the academic staff as an R.E. teacher on a part-time basis. I gradually assumed responsibility for History and Maths also, and because I worked in the secondary sector, this coincided with the advent of GCSE's which stipulated that the teacher was responsible for devising the questions for the new 'coursework' element of the exam. The coursework would comprise 25% of the overall grade. It was interesting but quite taxing. Not infrequently, I would be up until midnight and beyond marking books but I wasn't unduly troubled by this.

During a half-term break I went with my family for a week away to a Christian conference. During the second half of the week I became aware of a 'background' ache in my left eye. This persisted for several days and then 'erupted' until my vision in that eye became a fog. I went to see the Ophthalmologist at the hospital and he said it was rhetro -bulbar neuritis, a condition affecting the optic nerve for which there was no cure. He put me on anti-inflammatory drugs, and that was all. I was left with blurred and slightly impaired vision in the left eye. But more than that, the condition was aggravated when I encountered combative situations, which was not unusual for a teacher in a secondary school!

When I returned to school initially there were times when I could hardly see from one end of the classroom to the other. I remember clinging nervously to the rickety old staircase I had to ascend between lessons. The condition settled down a bit but I was left with some sight-loss in the left eye. The combination of these affects eventually drove me out of classroom teaching although I did a further couple of years of private tuition, after leaving school.

From the age of 22, when I became a Christian until the onset of this illness, I read avidly, but quite narrowly. I devoured biographies and autobiographies but they were usually spiritual or philosophical in nature. There was a deficit of ordinary literature.

As my ability to use my eye diminished, I began to read only what I deemed essential for lesson preparation and before long I was reduced to reading the back of the newspaper and the odd chapter of scripture. I stopped reading the Bible completely and invested in a set of tapes. This situation persisted for several years during which I fell in love with the poetry of Gerhardt Ter- Steegen, a German mystic who lived in the middle ages. It was wonderful to discover someone who articulates the language of your soul despite living centuries earlier in a different country!

Another writer I discovered at around the same period was Fredrick William Faber. I spent literally hours reciting and pawing over his poetry and his beautiful hymns. It felt to me that as a poet he surely must be without peer. I would sometimes recite verses of his poems to friends, who were sometimes quite grateful!

Of those in my own generation predictable names stand out. Bob Dylan, of course! I remember remarking to someone that he was incapable of writing anything that wasn't poetry! But I remember hearing that in the heyday of the hippie generation, around the time of the famous Woodstock Festival, Dylan was regarded by some as being the prophet and spokesman of the sub-culture, with anthems like, 'The Times They Are A Changing'. One star struck journalist approached him and said, "How far are you gonna' take this thing man?" He was appalled and replied (I paraphrase) "I don't know what you are talking about man, I'm just writing songs!" Whether he was naïve or oblivious his lyrics were latched on to by many as being inspirational, and whatever he thought - he was more a prophet than a commentator.

Another of my contemporary artists whose words were profound, and I found to be deeply moving was Leonard Cohen. He was able to express such beauty with his words, and also such pain. The latter was so powerful to me (such as in 'Bird on a wire') that I have had to stop visiting them. As I write these words, I recall just how fuelled I have been by all of those named, but it never occurred to me for one moment that I myself would ever be able to write poetry.

Poetry was easier for me to access at this time because it was often very short, so the amount of reading involved was minimal. And from my present vantage point I can see that my limitation may have proved to be a doorway for me.

By this time I had severed all my links with teaching as it aggravated my eye condition which was not just a localised limitation because it was an affliction of the nervous system. Sometimes it even 'hurt' me to speak. When I was first diagnosed with an inflamed optic nerve doctors were very grave and pessimistic toward me: "get a job with a pension", my GP advised. At 30 that was not good to hear. The implication seemed to be that the inflamed optic nerve was a doorway for something else. I was not willing to hear all this negative stuff spoken over me; not that I rejected what was said but I would not submit to it.

I had always been a believer in divine healing but, like many others with life-limiting illnesses, felt that it was something which God had allowed. Amy Carmichael in one of her books quoted a line from Ter-Steegen which read, 'Across the will of nature moves on the path of god. Not where the flesh delighteth, the steps of Jesus trod.'

Many times I had used this quote to make the point that God had allowed this. But it is a different thing to say that God allowed it than it is to say that he sent it, or that it is his will.

As the extent of my reading capacity diminished, I felt as though I was increasingly being shut down and in my desperation something within me said, NO! this cannot be right. I began to walk against the grain and resist the current that was seeking to swallow me up. This was faith militant, not passivity; rather like moving into the promised land. Gradually, with faith, I found that I was able to repossess some of the ground that had been stolen from me. As my faith continued to grow, I was able to dispense with my 'Bible on tape' and begin to read the scriptures normally again. Today, I am radically different from the time when I felt engulfed by a neurological paralysis. It is not perfect and I am still moving in and possessing my promised land.

This leads me on to the amazing revelation that I was able to write poetry myself. We were visiting our middle son Luke and his wife Elisabeth in France. Elisabeth is an artist and during the course of our conversation one day she asked if I had ever written poetry. I replied that I had not, and she asked me why not. "I have always felt it to be a bit above me", I responded. Maybe you should, she continued…

It was during this same visit, as we walked (trudged in my case) around one of Paris' many street markets that words of a poem began to drop into my mind. It was as though they had fallen from the sky! I was able to complete the poem by the time we came out from the market and by the time we returned to England had added a couple more. This was the beautiful genesis of my poetry!

CLIMBING UP

Rising the highest that we can go
Being the best that we can.
Learning from others so that we can know
The expression of his plan.

Walking uprightly throughout our days
Leaving no jagged edge.
Sweetening others upon their way
Keeping the word of our pledge.

Being the person I'm meant to be,
Unbribed, and not holding back.
To speak as I see, if others agree
Good! But the fear of man is a trap.

To keep pressing onward throughout my days
Not discouraged, but cutting some slack.
For others and me, so that grace we may see
Looking forward and then looking back.

EARLY FOR GOD

Early for God to get there first
To offer up the bad a worst

Early for God it has to be
I cannot find myself in me

Early for God this is the test
To offer up the good a best

Early for God the race is on
Not to the swift or to the strong

Early for God if you believe
Open your hands and you'll receive

Early for God don't miss the way
Or any word he has to say

Early for God, don't wait until
Tomorrow comes, to do his will

Early for God, the time is now
Just ask and he will show you how.

I HAVE SOUGHT

Through the trail of the haphazard
And the wastelands of fear
Through the contrary cries of reason
Through the dark lands of despair
Through the mirage of success
I have sought: is someone there?

From the maze of the subjective
And the land of broken dreams
Through the hopes of many decades
At last. I have come home
I've no need to seek asylum
Here they understand my language
All my alibis are past.

From the haunting land of mirrors
To the place of God's forgiveness
From the cold dark shadows cast
I had rowed my own boat early
But now I've gathered so much baggage,
That I cannot raise my mast.

Not celebrity, not glamour
Not a mirror held up high
Not great human achievements;

Unrelenting sacrifice;
Always seeking, never finding;
Longing...hope not realized.
Then a voice asks, "Who am I?'

So, I sought him in the desert
Someone said he is out there
And I sought him in the mystery
Someone said they'd make it clear
And I sought him in a garden
And I found him on a beach
And I laid my life before him!

I regard 'I have sought' as my signature poem because it symbolises some aspects of my journey; and I was converted on a beach!

UNTANGLING

What I am decides what you see
And what you see comes later.

What I say decides what you hear
But what you hear may be different.

What I say expresses what I mean,
Even when no one is listening.

What I believe informs what I do
But what I do can vary
The gap between such friends as these
Can get a little bit scary.

THE BLOATED SCIENTIST

Science is the discovery
Of what has been before.
But what is, compared to what is seen
Always amounts to more.

The claim to understand what is
Must leave an open door.
To shut the door and lock it up
Is science, no more.

To strut across the floor and shout
'No mystery I see!'
Is to proclaim, an ignorance
Amazing in degree.

The discovery of some new truth
Should make us seek for more.
And humbled by the knowledge say,
'We're still so very poor'.

YOUTH

If you aspire to be young
You'd better make a few more mistakes.
I had learnt to protect myself
Now I've learnt to expose myself.
Risky business living!

There's a poise, and a confidence,
Not born of experience
But still worthy of emulation
By those of us who have grown
Worried and neurotic, with the passing of years.

Instead of looking up we've looked down.
Their smile has become the rebuke
To our frown, who have looked nowhere.

THE GAME!

On the terrace in a football crowd
Throats croaking, voices loud
And tandems blare out mercilessly
And you are waiting, waiting, waiting,
For the game to start.

Anticipation builds, hope swells
Expectation growing constantly,
Atmosphere a full-term pregnancy
And still you're waiting, waiting, waiting
For the game to start.

The seats they fill up row by row
The stewards show us where to go
Faces blank; eyes glazed over
Conversation tense, minds focussed
And still you're waiting, waiting, waiting,
For the game to start.

Sometimes in life you have to wait,
I've been left standing at the gate
Or shut outside; confused and in the dark
But still I'm waiting, waiting, waiting
For the game to start.
Have I missed something?

I have been counselled by God that in writing poetry I must be completely honest and not conceal myself in ambiguity. But occasionally one must make a choice between ambiguity and non-disclosure, so I call this 'necessary ambiguity'.

WHAT WILL DEFINE YOU

Is it the morass of accumulated data held on a computer?
Surely that couldn't lie?
Or is it the wounds inflicted through painful experiences?
Is it the complements of friends or strangers?
Or the affection expressed or unexpressed by those close to you?
All of these may play a part but only God can define you..
To define is to limit.
He only knows our 'going out and our coming in', and is
'acquainted with all our ways'
When you are measured on his scales you will not be found wanting.

THE SUPERMARKET

A stranger am I within the crowd
Where faces are blank and voices are loud
And each rushes on toward their goal
And nothing is lost except the soul
In everything.

I mingle among the jostling throng
My numbness acute, the queue is long
Erect like a sentry, fixed my gaze
I'm nearing the exit of this maze
Of emptiness

So, rush on rush on, the time is set
The goal defined the deadline met
You cannot afford to fall behind
Or one will replace you in the line
Of senselessness!

I'm lost now, as carried on a sea
To where I do not want to be
Where nothing is gained and nothing lost
And nothing is traded here
Except for sanity

LOVE IS NAKED

Love is naked so keep it warm
Safe from the overarching storm
Keep it in a secret place.
Allot to it a special space
As new, and still unworn

In one of my very early flats, when I was about eighteen, I wrote and cut out the first line of this poem and stuck it on my wall. I have since added the 4 succeeding lines.

THE POSTURING OF HUMANITY

The posturing of humanity
I guess it had to be
The coding and the messages
Lest other eyes should see
Like 'Tinks' or like Jimmy,
Or the birds up in the trees.

The distance of humanity
Like seats set out apart.
The carefully concealing
Of what lies in the heart
It's sad, and its confusing
And I suppose you'd call it art.

The gambling of humanity
That time just carries on
That all the cold dark winters
Will end with summer sun
Till the whistle blows to call the end
Of what has not begun

I wrote this poem while waiting for Sadie, a gardener who worked for me, 'Tinks' was her cat and Jimmy an overbearing neighbour.

BUSYNESS

We stride forth confidently into another day
Busy with the stuff of life; relationships and play
Our tails are up, our headlights blaze, our diaries are full.
'Give place to me', 'I'm in a rush I cannot now delay'.
Tenuous, so tenuous, it will all be swept away.

A boy crafts his first sandcastle with turrets all around.
He adds a moat and fills it with a bucket from his hand
A second castle, then a third upon his grand estate
Puts soldiers on each turret; but the hour is getting late
Feverishly he digs the sand to hold the waters back
But one wave from the returning tide will knock his castles flat.

Our plans are big our gaze is strong our focus very clear.
We hold tomorrow in our grasp and even the next year
We hope for a promotion (and surely that's not wrong?)
Our hard work has rewarded us with prospects very strong.
And he who grants us our next breath asks, 'Didn't you know how long?'

I hold aloft a flag for hope, I hold a flag for peace
The wind unfurls it perfectly, when coming from the east.
I hold aloft a flag for life, I hold a flag for death.
And none can take his place down here, until he's granted breath.

I wrote 'Busyness' whilst on holiday with Luke and Elisabeth in France.

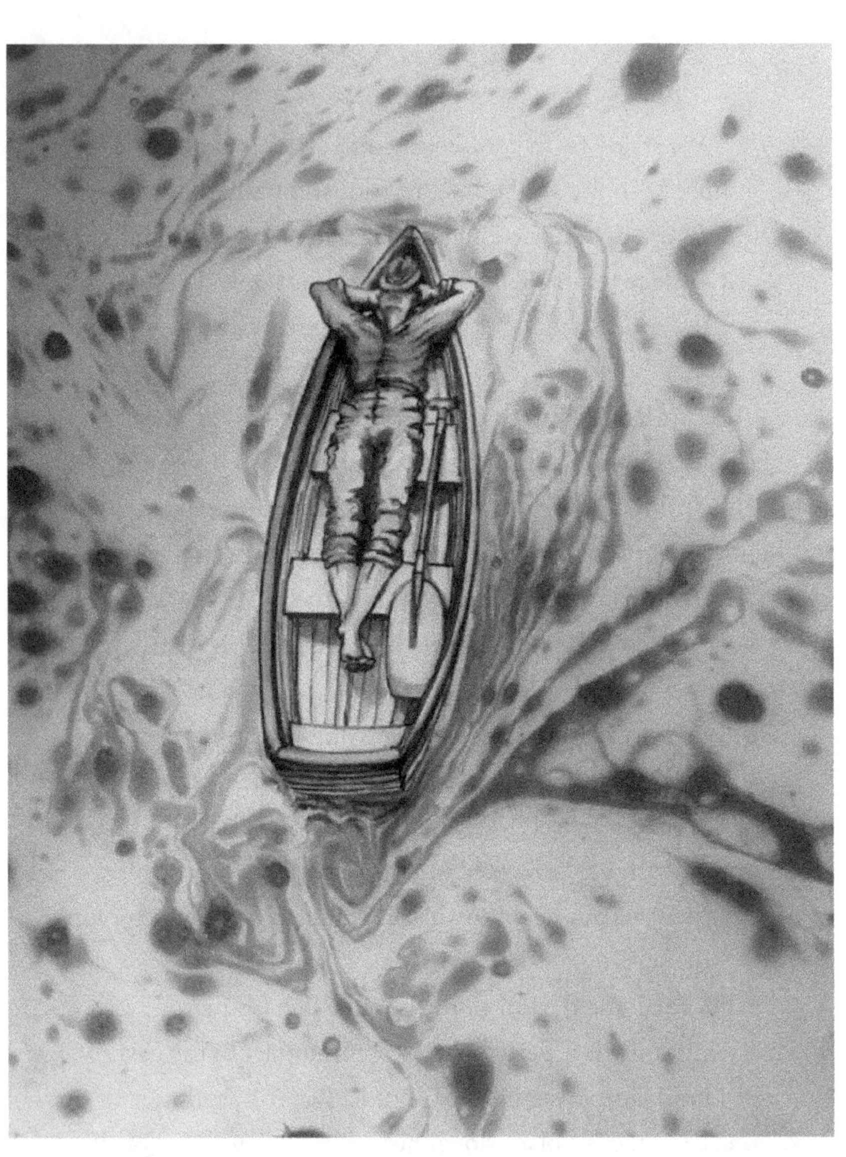

MERCY

Afloat on the sea of God's mercy
Not striving or seeking to be
Just resting, enjoying the moment
That kindness has brought to me

I know it can still get tempestuous
The wild raging elements
Scorning appeasement
All threaten to swallow me up!

But here in the now I find mercy
And amazement, that I should be free.
To express how I feel
And admit what is real
And trust for what I cannot see.

Fair is a word I find perplexing
My saviour was nailed to a tree
No trade off for him
Who bore all my sin
Justice cannot define love

Now I'll get in my boat and start rowing
And I'm moving before I can row!
Or I'm rowing without even moving!
And what I have reaped I will sow.

SILENCE

Silence is an empty place
Where fears and worries grow.
The gnawing pains of loneliness
That just refuse to go.

Silence is a scary place
When knowledge is denied
The mind runs over possibilities
The ocean wide.

Silence is a testing place
Where we must sit and wait
Knowing that just one word
Can another world create.

Silence is a healing place
For those who knock the door
And wait 'till they're invited in
To heavens treasure store

Silence is a waiting place
Where we can travel home
And realize that in this world
We are not alone.

Silence is the place of strength
Where we must come again
And touch the one who sends us out
Upon our way again.

SOBER REFLECTION

Playing fast and loose with destiny.
Our lives hang by a thread!
I'm feeling very mindful now
Of things I've thought and said.

The swagger of self-confidence
Now leaves a hollow taste.
Consciousness of image
Was nothing but a waste…

Of time; the prime ingredient
Which to the exit hastes,
And doesn't offer guarantees,
Or fables about fate.

And we are carried hostage
By things that we call friend.
Which pedal the illusion
That the circus will not end.

But end it must, as we move through
Into a faster lane.
And looking back, we hope, can say,
" I have not lived in vain!"

I composed this whilst hovering in the precincts of some hospital.

PRIDE

Self- promotion self- promotion
Stand out from the crowd.
Say it once and say it twice
And say it very loud.

Taking part in social discourse
Impassioned in my plea.
Concerned that all should get the point
That it's really about me! me! me!

Hello pride my close companion,
Enemy and friend.
When I'm sure of where I come from
All your power shall end?

'GRACE TO IT!'

We are the indebted ones
The record book will show.
That our attempts at righteousness
Just made our trespass grow!
We tried to swim against the tide
The force of nature to defy.

It proved too strong, and mastered me;
Flatly refused to set me free
A fugitive was I for years
Until the love of God appeared

A generous love, which has a breadth
Much greater than I know.
Which overtakes me on my way
When I am walking slow

"Move over now", he said to me,
"You're steering but you cannot see
The way that you should go".
My faith was real, but very weak,
And I was in the driving seat
But he came and gave me more!

If there's a cost, I could not pay
If there's a love I cannot say
Who sent it to my door.
No virtues here to qualify
That I should live and he should die.

THE BATTLE

Enough for me, oh surely not!
This seething, restless tide
Of desires disclosed and undisclosed,
And needs, the ocean wide.

I don't know if I'll pass the test
Convince the one who loves me best
That my devotion's true.
I fear that I shall wander out
Led by the passions of the flesh
To seek a better view

The battle is intense for me
I can't deny it's true.
A force more powerful than I
Determines what I do.

I cannot just say no to it
But I can say 'Yes' to him.
Who by the power of his love
Can lead away from sin.

For those who overcome, he said,
If they be rich or poor;
Shall find a place within his house.
And shall go out no more.

SOMETIMES

Sometimes I am carried.
Sometimes I fall down
Sometimes I am cushioned
From troubles all around.

Sometimes I am hurried
Sometimes I walk slow.
Too often I assume
That others, know where to go.

Sometimes I am hasty.
Sometimes I break rank
Sometimes I open fire
When I should 'bring up the flank'.

Sometimes I can show my face
Sometimes I must hide.
Sometimes an ill placed word from me
Can wound and divide.

We've all been given power
To injure or to heal.
To lift up, and gather in what's lost;
Or to disperse and steal.

Our lives made up of moments.
Too many have been lost:
With ill- advised and hurtful words
Lord, help us count the cost.

For this is the arena
Where we must win or lose.
While we still have the luxury
Of time: then let us choose.

PSALM 126

The dream of normality, what can it be?
How I aspire to what I cannot now see!
The sweet taste of freedom from duty and rote
The inner soul music that strikes up a note
For freedom.

The end of captivity, do I still recall?
The feelings, emotions, prior to my fall.
Now I am a prisoner, without the recourse
To justice, normality, laughter and hope.

I can't overstate the trauma you feel
When nothing around you seems common or real
And you can't recognise the place you now live
Or the person who lives there; can nobody give,
An answer?

For those who have fallen must be lifted up.
If they have drunk deep of the desolate cup
They will also drink deep of the unsullied joy
Of redemption and pleasure without alloy.

For each bitter herb there's a secret repose.
A sweet fragrant ointment which nobody knows
Applied by the hand from which you once roamed

And now draws you back to your heavenly home.

I wrote this poem in Turkey, with my wife Viv and friends Ges and Ruby.
It was a flashback to the torment and captivity of years gone by.

UNITY

I say disparate you say diverse.
You say it's better;
I think it's worse.
Us Protestant Christians
We're on the march.
But where are we going?
Nowhere fast!

We're fighting a battle:
A cause to declare.
Our rules of engagement
In common we share.
We know we can only
Move forward in prayer.
And that's the extent
Of our unity here.

An anarchic people
It should never be
A unity bought
So that others might see
The spoils of a victory
The conquest of love.
A signpost that points
Unto heaven above.

EATING FISH ON THE PONTOON

I have become a heaven tourist;
Finding the places where heaven touches earth.
Filling the spaces where rote becomes mirth.
Finding the joys which once had eluded me:
Taking the path back to simplicity
Eating fish on the pontoon.

Sell all your tickets; this beauty will pay you more.
Discovering something that you may have known before.
Recovering loss; and time spent which made you poor.
Prospecting for gold long buried in days before.
Eating fish on the pontoon.

Bow to the silence; invite it all over you.
Yield to the one who wants to steal up on you.
Catching you out (there's nothing to prove in here).
Just you, yourself, and a presence so very dear.
Bathe in the quiet; this moment is always new.
Accept all the good that he wants to do for you
Eating fish on the pontoon.

I wrote 'Eating Fish on the Pontoon' in retrospect, after travelling to Turkey to sell our house. Several evenings we ate fish with our friends out on the lake.

LOOK AWAY FROM YOURSELF

In this world of cool receptions
In this day of sad reflections
In an age of introspection
There's warmth coming from Jesus.

In the place of resignation
Hope deferred and hesitation
Amidst the noise and speculation,
There's hope coming from Jesus.

In this world of poor connections
Empty seats, unanswered questions
Hurtful words and cold rejection
There's love coming from Jesus.

Facing an abyss of darkness
Rushing forward, heedless, reckless;
Dulling pain ignoring heartbreak
In the eyes of Jesus.

Out in the cold a door is knocking
Quiet, persistent.
Here inside the fire is cosy
Familiar grief, friends that know me
As the person I am not.

Should I get up?
It’s become too easy to ignore it;
Fear and joy compete within me.
My heart races. Tears well up.
Come in my familiar stranger

THE FALL

Once relentlessly positive
Now plunged into a mist.
Don't know how I got here
What kind of place is this?
All places sacred.
No spaces empty.

Intolerant of everyone and everything
Phone won't answer, texts keep coming, clothes won't fit!
What kind of place is this?
All places sacred.
No spaces empty.

Swept as by a current
I gaze back at control.
The familiar vanquished
What kind of place is this?
All places sacred.
No spaces empty.

Normality questioned by my busy pen.
Oh, please come back to me
My dear rejected friend.
What kind of place is this!
Don't know how I got here

Not going to stay here.
All places sacred.
No spaces empty.

While courting the abyss
In moments, once, remiss
What darkened place is this?
I know how I got here
I'll never return here
All places sacred.
No spaces empty

A table spread before me
By which I am fed;
Not heavenly manna
But the living bread.
The voice calls me onward
(I'm not going backwards)
This place is sacred
No spaces empty.

In 2115 with huge reluctance I consented to a course of chemo-therapy It went on for about 8 months and I continued working. I was wonderfully helped during this period but the steroids had a very disorientating affect upon me and once, early in the treatment I contracted a minor infection, which is the context of these graphic experiences.

WAITING

The flowers lift their heads expectantly
At the sound of rain
They've waited long and patiently
With hope that does sustain.

A gentle touch, a deluge now
Is falling from the skies.
It feels like resurrection day
Without it they will die!

And I can learn a lot from these,
Upon my window-sill
That encapsulate the beauty
And the art of standing still.

THE WORD

A small man in a vast universe
Speaking clever words;
Wanting to be heard.
Forgetting my smallness,
Asserting my knowledge,
Not hearing natures word.

Disturbing the chaos
Imparting the fullness
Emptiness absurd!
I bow to the mystery
I sing with the voices
Of music still unheard.

Out of the silence
And primeval stillness
Rejoicing peeled the skies.
On creations morning
The spirit was moving
Unseen by human eyes.

Bestowing the order
With beauty and grandeur
No accident here!
Creation inspiring

With wonder untiring
Our gratitude here.
Our songs and our poems
Our art and our writings
Respond to the One.
Who once spoke creation
With great celebration
And then the music began.

NAT

May the music of your love play loud for him
May it sound above the crowd.
May it always form the backdrop
When he's called to take the stage
May it always find him ready
When it's time for curtain raise.

May the music of your love play loud for him
May it never be drowned out.
At the back of every whispered prayer
At the front of every shout.
When the affairs of life converge
With a loud and clattering sound
Grant him quiet in his spirit
And a peace that's so profound.

May he run and not grow weary
In the race that you define.
May he be kept whole in body
And sound within his mind.
May the music of your love play loud for him
May it sound above the crowd.

Our youngest son Nat began a course in Theatre studies. This Was my prayer for him.

THE MOVING LANDMARKS

Familiar locations bring solace to the soul.
All of them contribute a sense of being whole
We wend our way, along life's paths, unthinking 'cos we know,
Where we have come from; and where we think we'll go.

We boastfully assert ourselves, we jump and clap our hands
While life's stationery landmarks define just who I am.
Our claims of independence are hollow, and at best,
Will lead out from our harbour; will lead out from our rest.

But when there is a shifting of the tectonic plates
Or where there is a shaking of windows, doors and gates.
We cannot see outside ourselves; we cannot find the door
Or that precious thing we trusted in; we're shaken to the core.

For life will not stay static; you can be sure of that;
Though things may stand still long enough for you to take a snap.
So pose today with those you love and smile with those who can;
And travel on towards the arms of him who said, "I am".

PSALM 121

Every man's life is an enigma;
To himself, and to everyone else!
We live in a mystery. Life itself is a mystery.
We all need a great deal of help!

But where to look is the question?
Who can fathom our manifold ills?
Or the competing attempts to define us.
Shall I lift up my eyes to the hills?

There is just one way to resolve this.
In our exile, and in our return.
A preserver from our self-destructions.
A still place from which we may learn.

We are spinning around in confusion.
We can't always locate the ground.
We are looking but not always seeing.
He will not suffer your foot to be moved.

We are tortured and barely surviving,
As questions arise in our head.
When we shout them out loud we discover;
Our maker has not gone to bed.

I wrote this during the period that I was feeling 'a bit undone'. I had been believing God regarding a lump on my chest, but through circumstances (!) agreed to have it medically removed. My faith that I am healed by Christ remains unchanged; but I was experiencing the inevitable discomfort and minor incapacity which follows such procedures.

MOSAIC OF SUCH BEAUTY

A mosaic of such beauty sprang out from the dull tedium
Of my weary psyche; like a sudden fusion of colour upon
A grey landscape.
But what gave rise to such a dramatic contrast?
Was it a visitor from my sub-conscious sent to inspire,
Or galvanise me out of my inertia?
Or an escaped memory from the past, disembodied from it's
Original context? None of these seemed to really do it justice.
Colours so bright pass through the night of sorrow;
Penetrating anxiety and introspection. The distance is long
But the journey is short. On the boundaries of time no reason
Or rhyme discernible!
Not how far but how near! Not remote, and how dear
The hand that has mapped my journey.

I believe that this emerged from the period when I was on steroids, following my treatment in hospital.

LOUDLY BLEST

Loudly blest, quietly test the waters;
The hand of god.
Largely undetected by the hungry eyes of man
Our murmurs get louder our hearts become prouder
As we demand that God plays his part in the orchestra
Directed by ourselves.
But he has his own song that he is composing on our hearts.
We would do well to learn it!

A FIXED POINT

The malaise of relativism, affliction of our age.
Are you moving forward? Are we on the same page?
Now, who moved the goal posts? Did you score a goal?
Did the ball cross the line? Would you gamble your soul?
Now, what really matters, can anyone speak
Of truth unchanging, to find what you seek?
Our perceptions may vary and alter a lot
But 'I am the Lord I change not'!

JOINING UP

Time is an unbroken continuum
We experience it as divided into fragments
As 'day', as 'night', as 'work' as 'play'
But what we have done is what we do
And what we do is who we are
There's a rhyme and a rhythm and a reason to be
Excited by hope not irrelevancy;
For though time marches on, and the masses deny,
Politicians debate, while the nations cry:
For one to stand up with compassion and faith
Not intimidated by the politically correct agenda;
Not bending with the winds of intellectual fashion;
For truth stands indifferent to my agreement or acquiescence
Not depending on popularity to make its case,
Not deferring to pressure or contrived disgrace,
Not turning, but running full pace,
The race for freedom, integrity, fairness…
And justice on behalf of those…
Who have no voice, or whose voice isn't heard,
Not complicit by silence but speaking the word.

MUM

Laughter and tears
Roll back the years
Memories come flooding in.
Things that remain
Masking the pain
Of sorrow and loss.

But a flavour remains
Of one who was always
Generous, cheerful and kind.
This person lives on in our minds

For who can express
The value of one
Who touched our lives so tenderly.
Who coaxed us and taught us
Her mad priceless art
This person lives on in our hearts.

And we do not grieve
Like others who find
No hope beyond the grave
...We've inherited more than a space
Once again ,we will look on her face

What's committed to God
He will save.

I wrote 'Mum' to be read at my mum's funeral.

GRATITUDE

God has provided my every need
Shade on the balcony so I can read
Goats on the mountains to help me see
The value of freedom.

In what seems just random a pattern I find.
When my thoughts all tend downward I renew my mind
If darkness descends it can never obscure,
The path that leads onward.

I wrote the following whilst on holiday with Viv in Greece
Immediately following my graduation from Bible college.

IT'S NOT ABOUT ME

Your Word Is Truth
How far I have walked
How much I have talked
What sights I have seen on the way!
I've 'been there' and 'done that'
And am wiser today!!

Don't baptise your cynicism
And give it a name!
There's a dust- bin for all your arguments
And sincerely held objections
It is called the cross.
Maybe, you need to visit it?
I'll meet you there!

Thank you Jesus, for the quiet places of beauty you grant us.
Where the air is clean and the day is bright and solitude reigns.
Every Jesus space is a happy place.
Where our feet touch earth it's a Jesus space.
Help us to remember.

For we should not be like Jacob
Surprised that you are there.
And yet your love does surprise us:
Steals up upon us in unexpected ways,
And in familiar places,
Where, like Jacob, we ought not really to be!

*Viv, Mishka and I spent 3 days at the New Forest and met up
With Dick and Sandy. Amidst the sweltering August heat, I discovered a
cool tranquil seat at our guesthouse!*

DISTANCE

Distance is a scary thing
The alarms go off. The birds all sing.
It steals up unannounced.
Just when we thought that all was well
Like some great cat it pounced!

The birds have fallen silent now
Their voice can not be heard.
No early song, I listen hard,
But I cannot catch a word.

The thief is very busy now
He creeps up in the dark.
A house that once was full of joy
Is left exposed and stark.

Closeness is a precious gem
Prospected from the ground.
I didn't notice when it left
But it will come again.

So we must all stay vigilant
And hearken to his call.
--Not complicit in our fall
--But holding that redemptive hand

That leads us to a better land.

I wrote 'Distance' after receiving a letter from my daughter, who I had sparse contact with.

TIME

Time exacts a heavy toll
None exempt when they call the roll
No name missing
All are wishing
That they were elsewhere!

Successful men are at a loss
What once shone bright is now but dross..
Left on the shelf as a memento
For future generations.

But what defines success is a story to be told
Not the presence of the young or the domain of the old
The extent to which We've heeded the inner voice

TIME (2)

Life is here and now with god
And what is in between
The future is a distant land
Which cannot now be seen

While I enjoy the present
And what already is.
Others plan for coming days
But this one they will miss.

The time is always now
It shall not pass away.
It came with you and travels on
Through all your busy days.

Enjoy it as a gift
And don't wish it away.
And do not miss a single note
Of the anthem it will play.

The time is always now!
The place is always here
The way is always onward
And love is always near.

SPACES

I spend much time occupying spaces:
It's precious; it's my leisure, it's not a blank!
The silence ministers to my spirit.
Space is where I find myself

It's in engagement that I get lost!
Then I spend other periods filling spaces
This is the more challenging part!
The risk of being over-represented

And of speaking too much
And of occupying other peoples' spaces.
That is a real discipline.

PLEASURE

The morass of neutral and harmless things
Which divert our focus from the One thing!
If we live on the periphery we may become peripheral!
Our pleasure exists in the knowing and loving of God
Not in surfing the boundaries of what is permissible!
It is for his pleasure that we were created, not our own!

I received 'stick' from some people about 'pleasure'.
'Too austere and graceless', would be a paraphrase of the objections!

THE LOCKDOWN

A strange inertia has settled over me
An indecision walked in a captured me
The changing landscapes have left us all confused
We've lost our routines and just obey the rules
Self-preservation exerts a powerful pull.
We march in line, like soldiers on parade.
We must keep rank, the rules must be obeyed.
All art is dead! A reef has now been laid;
But from great loss, we trust we shall be saved.

Be saved we must, if we would contemplate
The full extent of our potential loss.
Our freedoms come at much too high a cost.
We bow the knee to what we value most
But in this time that's given to reflect,
And turn our thoughts to what we have neglected
And fill that space with Jesus, once rejected.

I wrote the previous poem during the 'Covid lockdown', in 2020.

THE COMPASS

How did I arrive here? It can be hard to say.
The consequence of hopes and dreams that happened on the way.
To imagine now with foresight, that I would land up here
I would have pressed the accelerator and moved up through the gears.

But where we are is here today, on this small piece of land
We cannot trace the process, or identify the hand,
That interwove the pathways to cross in such a way
The motives and the hungers that control us, as they may.

As we reflect and look around we like to see a plan;
Emerging from the chaos, a wave upon the sand
A footprint on the sea-shore, the waves will wash away
And if we're quick we can declare that, 'I walked here today'.

But we are not just victims of hostile circumstance:
The cold winds of evil, or the warm breath of romance
And we must not stay passive, or engage in idle talk
But looking to our compass, pick up our bags and walk.

About The Author

Mike Clark, a religious studies Teacher, Baptist Minister and gardener, living with my family in Worthing, west Sussex.

www.ingramcontent.com/pod-product-compliance
Lightning Source LLC
LaVergne TN
LVHW052057160826
845678LV00015B/3268